Overcoming Strongholds

"Walking Out Your Deliverance"

Apostle Dr. Tammy Morgan

ISBN: 10:1-946106-05-4
ISBN-13: 978-1-946106-05-6
Breakthrough to Glory Ministries
apostletammi@gmail.com
(revised 2019)

DEDICATION

I dedicate this book to those who are praying, and believing God for deliverance from personal struggles and strongholds.

CONTENTS

Overcoming Strongholds

~HERE I AM~

A few years ago the Lord placed on my heart to write a "how to" guide based on deliverance. He simply instructed me to keep a daily journal of my process. Never in my wildest dreams did I think my process would develop into a book. Deliverance is a one on one process. You may be feeling like you are the only one with some deep rooted desires, pain, and or hurts. You may feel like God has forgotten about you. You may be thinking that your struggles are so deep that deliverance is so far from your reach, but I'm here to tell you deliverance is for you! God has a plan for your life! God is waiting on us to call on Him. How do you call on

Him? You call on Him out of an honest and sincere heart. Your process is between you and God. I can only teach you what I know will work, and my friend I know this process works because it worked for me.

How many times have I cried out to God and asked God to touch me with his mighty hand of deliverance? I can't even count the times, but it wasn't until I started to seek God earnestly for some answers. The desire to have more of Christ and less of me in my day to day journey led me on the road of deliverance. I believe the Holy Spirit revealed to me that deliverance just doesn't happen without first acknowledging first we are nothing without Jesus, Only through

Him can we do all things, *"I can do all things through Christ who strength me."* Philippians 4:13* Paul wrote *"When I go to do good, evil is present." Romans 7:21*

Walking out your deliverance starts with faith. Paul wrote, *"Fight the good fight of faith,"* you have to believe that Jesus is your deliverer, and He will deliver you. Stay in the fight because you win! Jesus has already finished and won the fight for you!

Your next process is a total surrender to God, allow Him to do the work, *"Submit yourselves therefore to God. Resist the devil, and he will flee from you. (James 4:7)* If I had a dollar for every time the devil tried to get me to give up, I would be a billionaire today!

Seriously I submit my thoughts, my actions and my feelings to God every day. I want to encourage you to stand strong in your faith, hold your position regardless to how bad things may look, or how you may feel; know that Jesus will never leave you.

PRAYER

THANK YOU HEAVENLY FATHER FOR LOVING ME SO MUCH! I SUBMIT MYSELF TO

YOU, MY MIND, MY FEELINGS AND MY THOUGHTS. LORD, HELP ME THROUGH THIS PROCESS AS I WALK OUT MY DELIVERANCE.

In order to understand the process of deliverance, we first must understand the definition. According to Webster, deliverance is the act of delivering, liberation, or being rescued. When Jesus died on the cross He took everything with Him Hallelujah! You are totally free from all bondages! You are set free from the powers of darkness Hallelujah! In other words Jesus has already rescued you from all your personal struggles.

~The Deliverer~

Know who your Deliverer is. Your deliverer isn't your pastor; your deliverer isn't your mother or your earthly father.

Jesus is his name! God will use his servants to help you through these struggles, as he did with Moses.

"I am the Lord thy God, which have brought thee out of the land of Egypt, out of the house of bondage"

Exodus 20:2

Father God sent his son Jesus to this world to save, and to deliver us from the oppressor. And then He gave us the power to stand against principalities, powers, rulers of darkness and spiritual wickedness. Take the power God has given you to stand!

I want to share with you words from a great woman of God. As I walked through my process, I shared with her some of the struggles I was praying and believing God to bring me out of. She didn't say much, but what she said was so powerful. I will never forget those seven simple words; "Jesus is the one who will deliver." So simple, but so true! Often times we make the process harder than what it is. Sometimes the body of Christ rely on the pastor, the prophet, the evangelist, the teacher and the apostle to do the work only Jesus will and can only do. He is the one who will heal and deliver you from the spiritual strongholds. *"He is the King of Glory, strong and mighty."*

~THE PROCESS~

It was in small church in Detroit Michigan when the Holy Spirit would start to reveal and answer some of my many questions regarding my struggles. There it was right in the Word of God! The law of sin! Struggles with lust, envy, bitterness, unclean thoughts, jealousy, un-forgiveness; just a few strongholds we war against on a daily basis. These are all the manifestations of the law of sin. I believe the Holy Spirit revealed this to me to introduce me to my next level of deliverance. The law of the mind, and the law of sin.

I want you to stay with me on this for a minute. The apostle Paul wrote, "But I see another law in my members, warring against the law of my mind." My friend there is a war going on, the law of the mind, and the law of sin. The Holy Spirit was teaching me I had to change my school of thought of how God sees me.

I was giving permission to the law of sin to hold me in bondage. Please don't misunderstand me, often times we hide our mess, our sin under *"the process"* and therefore we justify why we do what we do. I want you to know if you want more of God it's time to let the personal struggles go so you can receive your total deliverance.

It's time for the body of Christ to be real with their struggles and cry out for real deliverance.

~*Don't believe the lie*~

I allowed the devil to use the form of rejection to hinder my process. I allowed myself to believe the lie! But as I walked through my process the Holy Spirit revealed truth to me, it wasn't the spirit of rejection I had to overcome; it was the spirit of self-sabotage. I grew up believing the words others had spoken over me. Therefore, allowing the lie to shape my character into a vessel that wasn't pleasing to God. I would like to go deeper into the spirit of self-sabotage and what sin it produces, but for now I will stop here.

The Children of Israel cried out, and God heard their cry! Hallelujah!

"and the Lord said, I have surely seen the affliction of my people which are in Egypt, and have heard their cry by reason of their taskmasters; for I know their sorrows, I am come down to deliver them out of the hand of the Egyptians, and to bring them up out of the land unto a good land and a large, unto a land flowing with milk and honey; into a place of the Canaanite, and Hittites and the Amorites, and the Perizzites, and the Hivites, and the Jebusites." Ex 3:7-8

Many of you have cried out of a sincere desire for God to help, for Him to deliver you out of your current situations. I want you to know Jesus wants you to receive your deliverance. He wants you to walk in the full liberty. I believe the Holy Spirit is ready to meet you right where you are. To bring you out of bondage! To bring you out of your Egypt! Jesus offered Himself for your freedom, for your liberty, for your breakthrough!

Prayer

~ Father I thank you for truth, Lord help me through this process. Show me Lord how to seek you for my deliverance. Father I want to walk in the fullness of my deliverance, thank you Lord~

~THE NEXT LEVEL~

One of many things I have learned while on this journey is, deliverance is truly a process, a process you cannot rush, and there are different levels of deliverance. The first process begins when you accept Jesus as your Lord and savior; let's call this process level one. Level two is when you step into knowing who Jesus is and how much He loves you.

It wasn't until I attended a holiness church in Detroit Michigan when I experienced my next level of deliverance. I began to pray and study the Word to develop an understanding of what the Father exactly wanted me to know about walking in deliverance. The more I studied, and prayed, the more the Father was showing me, about ME. It was my time to deal with Tammy. I knew that the Lord wanted to free me from the strongholds that were blocking me from reaching my destiny.

~*It's Got to Be More*~

That Friday night in that small church in Detroit Michigan, I will never forget how the Holy Spirit introduced me to a higher level of deliverance. Deliverance from the desire law of sin, *"But I see another law in my members, warring against the law of my mind, and bringing me into captivity to the law of sin which is in my members."* Romans 7:23 Oh! This is what I've been searching for! This is what I've cried out to God for! Lord here am I Lord! I cried out to the Lord. But before I jump ahead let me first ask this question.

Have you ever asked the Lord what is deliverance? What do I need to do to walk in full deliverance? I know I have! Many times! I've researched and I've prayed for my own deliverance. I've even taught on deliverance; I've received my ministry training in deliverance. But until I understood my process of deliverance, I found myself frustrated and discouraged because of the lack of understanding and knowledge. I want you to know that you are not alone. Don't stop believing! And don't stop praying! *"Now faith is the substance of things hoped for the evidence of things not seen."*

We as Believers must hold on to our faith. We must continue believing the Word of God, and the promises of Yahweh. I've cried out many days and many nights not understanding the struggle within. Oftentimes I found myself believing the lie that the enemy wanted me to believe. Even as I write these words I remember how I prayed day and night asking the Lord "what's wrong with me? Lord why I can't get over this hump!" I was standing on His Word. I knew He had washed my sins away! I had no doubt in my mind that He promised me deliverance or in the power of His deliverance. But yet I still allowed the enemy to convince me that something was wrong with me. I thought I was unworthy of deliverance and I wasn't fit for ministry.

My friend, God's Word is true. He was bringing me into a deeper understanding of His power. Although the enemy was fighting me left and right, the desire to know and serve God was within my heart, the desire out powered what the enemy was saying about me. Regardless of what things look like in the natural, or what lies the enemy is trying to get you to believe, continue to have faith in the Word of God and don't stop praying. When

Jesus cried, "It is finished," your sins and your deliverance was finished as well! It was done and completed! He took everything you are struggling with to the cross. You have to believe it and receive your deliverance on a daily basis.

The Apostle Paul struggled as well, but it did not stop him, he pressed through the law of sin, *"I thank God through Jesus Christ our Lord. So then with the mind I myself serve the law of God; but with the flesh the law of sin* (Romans 7:25). Paul understood the process, *"O wretched man that I am!*

Who shall deliver me from the body of this death" (Romans 7:24).

The Father knows everything about you. He knows every secret thought and every act behind closed doors. Yes everything! But he still called you his child, and He does not make mistakes.

THE PROCESS STARTS WITH BEING HONEST WILL YOURSELF AND WITH GOD BY FAITH.

~Don't Stop Praying~

When did the spirit of rejection enter in? When did jealousy make its ugly appearance? When did fear step in? Acknowledging the struggle and the sin by laying them on the altar is how you start your process. Be honest with God by denouncing the sin, Lord I liked it (name it) but I don't want to do this anymore! No more excuses, you can't allow the law of sin to control your actions.

Do you know rejection, jealousy, fear and sin

HINDERS YOU FROM REACHING YOUR

NEXT LEVEL?

As I sought the Lord for the answers, to my many questions regarding my deliverance, the Spirit of the Lord took me to Exodus. As I read the word of God, the Holy Spirit gave me understanding of what it actually means when God speaks deliverance into your life. God told Moses, *"Go tell Pharaoh, let my people go. The word of God will never return to him void.* "Let my people go" is still being heard throughout the earth! The voice of God is powerful! Deliverance took place at the moment the Father spoke. *Every spirit must obey the voice of God.* Deliverance didn't just happen for the children of Israel when Pharaoh decided to release them, deliverance happened when God spoke. Pharaoh didn't have a choice but to let God's children go, but they had to go through the process.

"and it shall come to pass that whosoever shall call on the name of the Lord shall be delivered: for in mount Zion and in Jerusalem shall be deliverance, as the Lord hath said, and in the remnant whom the Lord shall call." Joel 3:32

~*Pray Until You Breakthrough*~

I remember the day I received my deliverance. I heard these words so plain and clear, *"it's enough"* after hearing these words my spirit went into a travailing prayer. As I prayed, I heard the Holy Spirit say so very softly turn to Mark 14:6. *"And Jesus said, Let her alone; why trouble ye her?"* This was the day God spoke deliverance into my life. Was I delivered that day? Yes! Did I have to go through a process? Yes! God spoke it, I received it, and now I had to walk through it. Regardless of how ugly it was going get, regardless to what I had to acknowledge, my day is here! Hallelujah!

Just like it was for the children of Israel, I had to walk through the desert for a season.

Overcoming Strongholds

Truth, prayer and faith is the

foundation to your deliverance!

~*YOU ARE NOT ALONE*~

The spirit of Pharaoh had to be defeated. Just like Pharaoh, the enemy doesn't want to let you go, and he will not go without a fight. When you confront and resist the devil with the Word of God, he doesn't have a choice but to let you go. Confront the spirit that's tormenting you and take the power of deliverance that God has for you! Close the door to the devil and open the door for God to work in you.

Moses believed God, and he acted

on what God instructed him to do, and
because of that, the yoke of bondage
was broken. You too have to believe.
You too have to act on the word of
God. How do you act on the word of
God? You praise the Lord for your
deliverance, you continue to stand on
the word of God by faith, and you turn
away from the struggle. No matter what
the enemy is trying to say about you,
trust God any way! The enemy will try
to steal what God has already given
you. The devil is lurking and waiting
for opportunities to plant seeds of doubt
and disbelief, but Jesus has given you

everything you need to fight back.

*"Stand fast therefore in the liberty
wherewith Christ hath made us free,
and be not entangled again with yoke
of bondage"*

Galatians 5:1

As I mentioned earlier, Paul had some struggles, but Paul understood the process; he was honest with God regarding his struggle. You have to get to this place in your prayers. Paul reached a point in his walk with God when he had to deal with the warfare in his mind that was drawing him to submit to the law of sin.

" for that which I do, I allow not; for what I would, that do I not, but what I hate, that do I. If then I do that which I would not, I consent unto the law that it is good. Now then it is no more I that

do it, but sin that dwelleth in me. For I

know that in me dwelleth no good

thing; for to will is present with me; but

how to perform that which is good I

find not. For the good that I would I do

not: but the evil which I would not, I

do. Now if I do that I would not, it is no

more I that do it, but sin that dwelleth

in me. I find then a law, that, when I

would do good evil is present with me.

For I delight in the law of God after the

inward man: But I see another law in

my members, warring against the law

of my mind, and bringing me into

captivity of the law of sin which is in

my members. O wretched man that I am! Who shall deliver me from the body of this death? I thank God through Jesus Christ our Lord. So then with the mind I myself serve the law of God: but with the flesh the law of sin."

Romans 7:15-25

~DON'T BE DECIEVED~

Deliverance is a death to the law of sin in your flesh and deliverance will only come when you cry out to God. Yahweh will only deliver you out of the sin if you want to be delivered. *"I beseech ye, therefore brethren that you present your body a living sacrifice holy, acceptable until God with is your reasonable service."* You have to present yourself to God first. He is a God of free will, He will never force His ways onto you. If you want a closer relationship with the Father, you have to resist the lie the enemy would persuade you believe.

~*Walking in your deliverance*~

One of the many things I love about our heavenly Father is His promise to never leave us! Not only does He love you enough to deliver you, but He gave you the power to fight the enemy back.

"For our weapons are not carnal, but mighty through God to the pulling down of strong holds."

~*Knowledge is Powerful*~

Overcoming Strongholds

When you overcome a struggle or a stronghold, you receive the knowledge of how that spirit operates. And with that knowledge you take away the power from that stronghold. You can smell it, you can see it, you can hear it, and you can feel the darkness of that spirit. When you are fully delivered, you can command that spirit to leave before it can manifest again. You also have the power and authority to pray for others to be delivered from that same struggle or stronghold.

Overcoming Strongholds

I'm not saying I have it all together and I don't fight against the law of sin. But I have been given the power to overcome the darts of the enemy. I will continue to walk out my process on a daily basis with the knowledge and understanding of how to hold on to my liberty. I will continue in prayer, I will praise and thank the Lord everyday for His mercy and His promise to keep me in perfect peace. When you stand firm and unmovable on the word of God and his promises you WIN!

~*Guard your Mind*~

"And take the helmet of salvation." Before I end, I would like to share one more thing with you. *"Casting down imaginations, and every high thing that exalteth, itself against the knowledge of God, and bringing into captivity every thought to the obedience of Christ; and having the readiness to revenge all disobedience, when your obedience is fulfilled."* 2 Corinthians 10:5

You have the authority through Christ against thoughts that illegally try to enter into your mind. Don't allow the thoughts to underestimate the authority you have been given. When the enemy brings a thought to your mind, his plans are to get you to submit to the law of sin. But you have the power to cast those thoughts down.

Captivity - the state of being captive

Captive - taken and held as prisoner, kept with bounds, held under control.

Prisoner- deprived of his liberty and kept under involuntary restraint.

The Father has given you the power to take those ungodly negative thoughts and keep them under control. Restraining those thoughts with Word of God. When an ungodly negative thought comes to your mind you have the power and authority to take that thought which was meant to imprison you, and imprison it. The word of God takes away the liberty from that ungodly thought and prevents it from manifesting. When you resist that thought you are literally telling the devil that your mind will no longer be his playground. No longer will unholy thoughts have liberty in your mind! No longer will you allow fear, hatred, and jealousy to rule you! No longer will bitterness and rejection stop you! And no longer will addictions control you!

~*Never Stop*~

Remember Jesus' desire is for you to walk in the full liberty of His Spirit. Stay in the word of God (the Word is your weapon). Stay in prayer. Be honest about your struggles and most importantly continue to believe in the promise, *"whosoever shall call on the name of the Lord shall be delivered."* If you continue on this path the strongholds you are struggling with will no longer be strongholds.

~Negative Thoughts exercise~

I pray this exercise will help you as
it helped me
get through my process.

Picture those negative thoughts as a baseball being pitched at you. Your bat is your weapon, (the Word of God), and you are in total control of the bat. When you see that ball coming at you take your bat (the Word) and swing back!

~NOTES~

~NOTES~

Overcoming Strongholds

~DAILY JOURNAL~

Overcoming Strongholds

~DAILY JOURNAL~

ABOUT THE AUTHOR

Apostle Tammy Morgan is the founder and CEO of Tammy Morgan Ministry and Breakthrough to Glory Ministries established November 12, 1997. Breaking Through to Glory radio ministry aired for the first time in Detroit Michigan, and later in Texas, GA, Tennessee, and some parts of Africa. As a Teacher and Apostle, Tammy travels to teach, equip and help others walk in their purpose and destiny.

Tammy has a unique and
peculiar anointing that brings
restoration healing, and deliverance to
the body of Christ. Tammy accepted
her call to apostleship through the
ordination and affirmation into the
office of an Apostle in 2013.

Apostle Tammy heart's desire is to
please God through her acts
of obedience to His Word and HIS will
for her life.   Because she has a heart to
serve God and His people, God
has opened many doors for Tammy to
teach, and equip the body of
Christ through the healing power of

the Holy Spirit. In 2014, the School of Ministry was established to train and to equip the Five Fold Ministers to go out into the vineyard.

www.ingramcontent.com/pod-product-compliance
Lightning Source LLC
Chambersburg PA
CBHW021146020426
42331CB00005B/928